Fashioning the Future
Blockchain's Impact on Textile and Design Markets

Table of Contents

Chapter 1. Introduction

In the crux of an unprecedented revolution, the realm of textiles and design is entwining with breakthrough technology called 'Blockchain'. Our Special Report titled 'Fashioning the Future: Blockchain's Impact on Textile and Design Markets' delves into this exciting confluence, carefully peeling back the layers of how Blockchain's transparent, immutable, and decentralized nature promises to reshape the industry's operations and ethos. Fear not the technical density of this topic. We've crafted this report with painstaking simplicity, making it invariably accessible for both seasoned tech mavens and the layman. Through meaningful insights and relatable analogies, it will artfully guide you through the radical transformations to anticipate, incorporate and potentially, lead. For lovers of fashion and aficionados of technology alike, this report is a vibrant tapestry of innovation and future potential waiting to be unfurled. Let's walk together through this pioneering junction where style meets substance, authenticity meets technology, and the future of fashion gets woven anew!

Chapter 2. Unraveling Blockchain: A Layman's Introduction

It was Thomas Edison who said, "To invent, you need a good imagination and a pile of junk." In the realm of cryptocurrencies and the blockchain, that "pile of junk" appears to be a bunch of hard drives and servers. The technological landscape has been rocked to its core by the advent of Bitcoin a decade ago and the underlying technology, the 'Blockchain'. While it can seem highly technical, blockchain can be a game-changer and is not as complex as it might seem at the outset. We now take a closer look at blockchain, from a layman's perspective.

2.1. Into the Blockchain: A Bird's Eye View

Simply put, a blockchain is a chain or sequence of blocks, where each block records information about transactions, just like a bank ledger. What differentiates blockchain from traditional ledgers is its transparency and decentralization. Every block of information ('block') is connected to each and every other block in the chain. Hence, the metaphorical 'chain' of 'blocks'.

Furthermore, each block is timestamped, with a copy of this chain existing on multiple computers across the globe, reducing the chance of fraud and making it accessible for all. For example, imagine an open ledger available in a public library where everyone could read all the entries but nobody could tamper with them.

2.2. Decoding Blockchain: Works and Operations

A closer look into the world of blockchain exhibits a fascinating union of technology and group dynamics. Let's dissect the basic principles that build a functioning blockchain system.

1. Decentralization: Unlike the conventional systems where one central authority like a bank verifies transactions, in a blockchain, group members collectively validate each transaction.

2. Immutability: Once a transaction is verified and added to the blockchain, it becomes immutable. Not even the person who made the transaction can alter it afterward.

3. Consensus: Before any modification, the blockchain network's members must agree to it, making it difficult to tamper with the information on the blockchain.

The mechanics begin with a transaction: person 'A' wants to pay person 'B'. This transaction is broadcasted to the network, where members verify its authenticity. Upon verification, it's added to a block. Blocks are then added to the chain sequentially, further authenticated with complex mathematical equations. This abstract string of operations is the core foundational principle of blockchain technology.

2.3. Blockchain: Beyond Cryptocurrencies

Although its most common application so far has been cryptocurrencies, the potential of the blockchain system is vast, ranging from smart contracts to decentralized supply chains.

In the context of textiles and design, integrating with blockchain could enhance product authenticity, streamline supply chains, and eliminate the need for middlemen. Integrating blockchain with textiles and design could create a new layer of transparency and trust between businesses and customers.

2.4. Facing the Challenges

Despite its revolutionary potential, blockchain still has challenges that need to be tackled. These include:

1. Accessibility: As we move towards implementing blockchain in various sectors, user-friendly platforms need to be developed for people devoid of technical knowledge.

2. Scalability: Current blockchain systems have limitations in terms of the speed of transactions, which need to be addressed.

3. Regulation and Control: As it is decentralized, it's difficult for any one entity to exercise control over it, leading to concerns about legality, digital rights, and taxation.

2.5. Conclusion: The Future is Here and Now

The future of blockchain technology indeed seems promising. From creating cryptocurrencies that challenge our understanding of currencies to transforming supply chain management, blockchain has potential for significant impact. Ensuring that we understand the basics and possibilities of blockchain is important because chances are that in the near future, blockchain is going to become part of our everyday life.

In essence, blockchain, as a platform, can provide an underlying layer of trust, transparency, and security - thereby making possible decentralized ways of doing business that were previously unthinkable. Truly, this is a leap from the centralized world we have known thus far to a world where trust and transparency become the new currency.

As we continue to investigate the potential of blockchain in the textile and design market, it's critical to understand that blockchain is more than just a technology to support cryptocurrencies. It is a system that may transform the way we engage in trade and industry, the way we buy and sell, and even the way we trust each other in a digital world.

Chapter 3. Blockchain and Fashion: An Unexpected Interweave

As we find ourselves at a pivotal juncture in history, a digital revolution is unfolding that promises to invigorate and reshape multiple industries. One such industry poised at the cusp of this transformation is fashion. Averred as the second-largest polluting industry in the world, the fashion industry is riddled with inefficiencies and inequalities ranging from opaque supply chains to counterfeits. As we get ready to delve into the labyrinthine intricacies of merging blockchain and fashion, it's crucial to understand the foundational aspects of blockchain technology.

3.1. UNDERSTANDING BLOCKCHAIN

At its core, blockchain technology is a type of database that records digital information (blocks) in a public or private network (chain). This information is inherently resistant to modification, providing transparency and traceability. Every transaction or record within a blockchain is confirmed by a network of computers (nodes), ensuring data integrity and thwarting tampering. Blockchain's antonymous relationship with central authority makes it a popular choice for peer-to-peer transactions and creating a decentralized digital economy.

How might this revolutionary technology catalyst change in the world of fashion and textiles, an industry known for its fluidity, artistry, and relentless pace? How might this unexpected interweave impact the creators, manufacturers, and consumers of fashion?

3.2. BLOCKCHAIN FOR ETHICAL AND SUSTAINABLE FASHION

As more consumers become conscious of the environmental and human ramifications of their purchases, the demand for ethical and sustainable fashion is rising. However, the complex and often obscure supply chains in fashion make it difficult to trace the origins of a product or validate a brand's claims about sustainability.

Blockchain can provide a solution to this issue. With its immutable nature, it can ensure data integrity and traceability from farm to finished product. Each step of production can be recorded on the blockchain, and consumers can easily inspect the journey their attire has taken, enabling ethical decision-making based on the supply chain information.

Additionally, with the potential to incorruptibly record certificates and credentials for raw materials, labor conditions, and energy use, blockchain can help validate sustainability claims and rally against greenwashing.

3.3. A SHIELD AGAINST COUNTERFEITING

The fashion industry, particularly the luxury segment, has been battling counterfeiting for years with little to no success. This is mainly due to the difficulties in tracking and identifying authentic products.

The unalterable, transparent nature of blockchain offers a potent tool to fight forgery. By registering products on a blockchain, brands can attach a digital identity or "token" to each piece of clothing. These digital tokens act as certificates of authenticity that can be accessed and verified at any time, making the detection of counterfeit products seamless for both vendors and consumers.

3.4. IMPROVING EFFICIENCY IN SUPPLY CHAINS

Blockchain can streamline various processes within the fashion supply chain, including sourcing, logistics, and payments. Since blockchain records are transparent and immediately verifiable, it can help overcome the challenges related to trust, hence streamlining agreements and transactions between disparate parties in the supply chain.

Moreover, by employing a type of blockchain architecture knowns as 'Smart Contracts', conditions of agreements can be pre-set and transactions can be automatically processed once these conditions are met. This not only shortens the time and reduces paperwork, but also minimizes the chances of fraud and dispute.

3.5. EMPOWERMENT OF ARTISANS AND DESIGNERS

Blockchain brings a promise of empowerment to creators. By recording designs on a blockchain database, designers can prevent illicit reproduction and affirm their rights to their creations.

Furthermore, blockchain-backed platforms can enable peer-to-peer sales, reducing intermediaries and allowing consumers to have a direct relationship with artisans. This not only ensures a fairer split of revenue but also fosters a community of trust and mutual appreciation.

3.6. FUTURE DIRECTIONS AND CHALLENGES

The intersection of blockchain and fashion indeed has the potential to redefine industry norms and bring forth much-needed change. Still, the journey is not devoid of challenges. Concerns over energy usage, the need for technical knowledge, and resistance to change are some bottlenecks that need to be addressed.

However, as we have seen time and again, the march of progress is seldom halted, and it certainly seems that Blockchain, with all its potential, is set to cause a stir in the fashion landscape, and rewrite the rules of the game. The fashion industry, just like the garments it produces, is about to be cut from a very different cloth. Innovation and future potential are taking center stage, defying convention and weaving a new narrative where art, technology, and ethics intermingle.

As the fashion industry prepares to dress itself in this new attire, the canvas for innovation is expansive, the threads of change are ready, and the loom of blockchain technology is set. Fashion, the epitome of evolution and reinvention, stands prepared to rewrite its own story, and it's a narrative that promises to be as enthralling as it is transformative.

Let's look forward to this inevitable, exciting future, a future where fashion marries technology to address its longstanding issues and create a sustainable, efficient, and fair trade. The day is not far when a designer in Milan will design a dress, a cotton farmer in Texas will be assured of his fair pay, an artisan in India will weave it, the garment worker in Vietnam will craft it beautifully, and a consumer in New York will wear it, knowing its entire journey. The future of fashion is not just about wear; it's about understanding, acknowledging, and valuing everyone involved in its creation. This is the future that blockchain can enable.

Welcome to the new world of fashion, a world that promises transparency. Welcome to the future, a timeless, fashionable future backed by the power of Blockchain!

Chapter 4. The Fabric of Transparency: Blockchain's Impact on Supply Chain

The current condition of the textile and design industries is encumbered with complexities and opaqueness, making tracking and transparency a daunting task. Blockchain technology, however, offers a promising solution to these challenges with its ability to bring about unrivalled degrees of transparency, immutability, and decentralization.

4.1. The Theoretical Framework: Understanding the Blockchain

Before delving into the specifics about the transformative effect of Blockchain on the textile and design sector, it's essential to comprehend its basic principles. Blockchain is a digital ledger of transactions that are duplicated and distributed across the entire network of computer systems on the Blockchain. Each block contains a number of transactions, and every time a new transaction occurs on the Blockchain, a record of that transaction is added to every participant's ledger.

Blockchain's decentralized nature ensures that no single entity holds the reins of authority; instead, all participants in the network have control. Furthermore, the immutability of a Blockchain, ensured by cryptographical algorithms, ensures that once data is added to the Blockchain, it becomes almost impossible to change.

4.2. The Right Thread: Blockchain's Role in Supply Chain Management

Applying this theoretical framework to the supply chain in the textile and design industries, Blockchain introduces a novel approach to transparency and authenticity. The technology can trace every step in the supply chain — from raw material sourcing, manufacturing to retail.

At the genesis of the process, Blockchain securely records all information related to the procurement of raw materials, including details of the source, cost, quality, and ethical information. This information block, once added, is now viewable for all participants, establishing an absolute and unalterable point of reference.

When the raw materials advance to manufacturing, a new layer of information gets added to the existing data block. This could include details about the manufacturer, time of manufacturing, machinery used, and a record of quality assurance checks.

As these goods navigate through logistical channels, each movement can be securely recorded on the Blockchain. When the product is finally retailed, the complete saga of its journey from source to shelf can be traced back in a tamper-proof data trail.

4.3. Unraveling Benefits: An Assurance of Authenticity

Eradicating counterfeit products remains one of the colossal challenges for the textile and design industry. Blockchain, with its immutable characteristic, combats counterfeits by providing a transparent trail of data that can be inspected at any point. This not only assures the customer of the product's authenticity and quality but also protects the brand's reputation.

Sourcing with a backbone of Blockchain also resonates with changing consumer desires. The modern consumer seeks out ethical and sustainable manufacturing practices; and transparent supply chains can validate these practices. Brands utilizing Blockchain demonstrate a commitment to ethics, attracting consumer trust and loyalty.

4.4. Challenges and Considerations: The Path Ahead

While the potential benefits paint a promising future, it's worth noting that implementing Blockchain technology in supply chains is not free of challenges. Achieving 'full transparency' requires all members of the supply chain — from raw material providers to retailers — to participate. Minor slips or errors during data recording could compromise accuracy. Technical literacy, financial costs, and data security are also significant considerations.

However, these challenges don't negate the enormous potential of Blockchain. Collaborative efforts and the development of practical frameworks can foster the right environment for the full-scale implementation of Blockchain.

In conclusion, the fashion supply chain stands on the cusp of a revolutionary overhaul. woven into the fabric of transparency, Blockchain technology is well-poised to shape the industry, promoting transparency, combating counterfeits, and resonating with conscious consumer trends. As unprecedented as the challenges may seem, so are the rewards waiting at the end of this pioneering journey. The much-needed transformation is undeniably complex, but it beckons an industry that is fair, transparent, ethical, and forward-looking. And who knows, maybe this is just the beginning of a truly stylish revolution of reformation.

Chapter 5. Sustainable Style: Blockchain's Role in Ethical Fashion

The world of fashion has always been marked with creativity, innovation and continuous evolution. However, it also holds a devastating track record when it comes to environmental sustainability and ethical practices. Production processes are often tainted by excessive waste, dangerous working conditions and extreme water consumption. This is a shadow side of fashion that increasingly conscientious consumers are unwilling to ignore. Blockchain, with its transformative power, is the perfect tool to bring transparency and accountability to this industry.

5.1. The Blockchain Revolution

Blockchain is a decentralized digital ledger, an immutable record of all transactions made within its system. Its transparency and immutability are the key attributes that can revolutionize sustainable practices within the global fashion industry. By establishing a traceable path from raw materials to finished fashion products, Blockchain can reveal the transparency regarding how, where, and by whom those products were made.

Each step in the production chain can be logged into the blockchain; from the sourcing of materials, through dyeing and weaving, right up to finished garment. It is the transparency and traceability facilitated by Blockchain that can help eradicate some of the most egregious ethical violations occurring in the industry.

5.2. Transparency and Traceability

Transparency refers to making information about the production process open and available. Traceability builds on this concept, adding the ability to track products from their creation to their final stage. Both together enable consumers to make informed decisions and encourage businesses to adhere to best practices.

By using blockchain technology, each level of the production process can be tracked, verified and logged in an immutable ledger. This creates a system where brands can't simply claim sustainability but must prove it. Blockchain's inherent transparency and traceability extend to the end consumer, providing full chain of custody and allowing consumers to make informed, ethical purchasing decisions.

5.3. The Power of Provenance

How does one discern whether a garment is ethically manufactured or merely marketed as such? It boils down to provenance, a detailed history of the origins and ownership of an item. Blockchain has the unique capability of recording unalterable proof of provenance.

The blockchain records an item's journey from its origin through its journey to the marketplace, tracking vital information like the material's source, workers' working conditions, and fair trade practices. This demystifies the often opaque supply chain, enabling consumers to make informed decisions and promoting honesty and sustainability in business practices.

5.4. Fair Trade and Ethical Consumption

Ethical consumption urges consumers to make purchasing decisions that align with their personal values. This can only be realized fully when consumers receive verifiable facts about the products they buy. Blockchain's ledger system holds brands accountable, providing consumers with facts rather than smooth marketing rhetoric.

For the trade to be fair, everyone in the supply chain, from the cotton farmers to the factory workers, must be paid a fair wage and work under decent conditions. Blockchain supports this vision by creating an unerasable history of every transaction, ensuring that every worker involved has been treated fairly and adequately paid.

5.5. Environmental Sustainability

Consumption and production in the fashion industry account for 10% of global carbon emissions. With blockchain, pollutants compliance, energy efficiency, GHG emissions at every stage from raw material extraction to final customer purchase can be tracked and verified accurately.

Blockchain can also register circular economy initiatives such as recycling or reselling clothes, as unique blockchain IDs can assure future consumers of the garments' history and its sustainable path.

In conclusion, the introduction of blockchain into the fashion industry offers a myriad of opportunities for sustainable innovation. It holds the key to establishing a new culture of transparency, traceability, and authenticity in the fashion industry. However, implementation is not without its challenges. Brands must invest in conjunction with other technologies to take the full advantage of blockchain's potential. But, with the rising demand for accountability and sustainability, embracing the technology may very well be the only way forward. Together, with informed consumers and innovative businesses, Blockchain can revolutionize the fashion industry, weaving a future where style and sustainability go hand in hand.

Chapter 6. Authenticity Unthreaded: Combating Counterfeits via Blockchain

A world blanketed in smart, intuitive fabric is no longer limited to the realms of fantasy – as the capacity of blockchain technology stretches beyond cryptocurrencies and into the folds of the textile industry, such innovation is touching reality. Whether to manage supply chains, prove authenticity, or nurture sustainable practices, blockchain is indeed fashioning the future. One of the most potent uses of this revolutionary technology lies in its ability to combat counterfeiting, a long-standing thorn in the industry's side.

6.1. An Epidemic of Counterfeits

The textile industry, particularly the luxury fashion sector, has been embroiled in an enduring battle against counterfeits. These faux creations not only taint a brand's prestige but lead to exponential losses annually. As per industry estimates, the global value of counterfeiting in the year 2020 was around $1.2 trillion, costing the fashion industry a staggering $600 billion.

The menace of counterfeits is expansive and multi-dimensional, affecting various stakeholders – from consumers deceived into buying low-quality knock-offs to corporations grappling with revenue losses and diluted brand image. Nipping this issue at its source requires holistic, reliable and innovative measures. And within blockchain technology lies the potent saviour, armed with mechanisms that can make counterfeiting a thing of the past.

6.2. Decoding Blockchain: A Brief Recap

Before we look at how blockchain can hold the counterfeit scourge at bay, let's revisit its core mechanics. In essence, blockchain is a series of 'blocks' (digital information) stored linearly in a public 'chain' (database). This digital information pertains to various transactions, with each block storing the details about the transaction, including date, time and the parties involved.

The security lies in blockchain's incorruptible and transparent ledger system. Each block contains a unique code - the hash, which changes with every transactional modification, making it practically unalterable without notice. Moreover, decentralized by design, blockchain's information is spread across not one, but countless computers – the combined computing power needed to alter this data is astronomical; hence, nudging the chances of hacking or fraud towards zero.

6.3. Fashioning Trust with Blockchain

Interweaving blockchain technology into fashion and textile industries poses radical solutions to the counterfeit problem. Its transparent, immutable, and decentralized nature brings a trifecta of attributes that together can significantly dilute the scope of counterfeits.

It all begins with a simple premise – imbuing each product with a unique digital identity that can be mapped and tracked across the entire value chain, making it effortlessly verifiable and thereby, resistant to fraudulent duplicity. This digital identity can be encrypted in the form of a QR code or an NFC chip attached to the product.

1. **Transparency**: Every step of the product's lifecycle, starting from raw materials sourcing, manufacturing, packaging, distributing to finally reaching the end customer can be recorded on the blockchain. This creates an open yet secure record-keeping infrastructure, where the origins and history of each piece can be traced back to its roots.

2. **Immutability**: Once information is stored within the blockchain, it cannot be tampered with. This crucial feature ensures the authenticity of the records, making counterfeits easily identifiable and verifiable.

3. **Decentralization**: Unlike centralized systems, where governance is concentrated in a single entity's hands, blockchain offers a decentralized model. This means that all stakeholders in the value chain can have a shared control over the information, making it resilient against singular points of fraud or failure.

6.4. Case Studies: Blockchain Combating Counterfeits

Several fashion brands have been early adopters of blockchain technology, experiencing its transformative potential in the quest against counterfeits.

*Paris-based fashion house, Martine Jarlgaard, made waves in the industry when they offered blockchain-protected clothing. With each of their garments embedded with a tiny NFC-enabled label, the entire journey of the product can be scanned and verified using a smartphone device.

Luxury giant, Louis Vuitton, has also rolled out its blockchain platform 'AURA.' AURA allows consumers to access the product history and proof of authenticity – including details on craftsmanship, raw materials, and points of sale – by scanning a unique code associated with each product. This not only assures the consumer of the product's authenticity but also educates them on the creative and ethical process behind it.

6.5. The Road Ahead

While the initial signs of blockchain's impact on combatting counterfeits are encouraging, the journey is still in its early days. Hindered by technological pitfalls and lagging industry adoption, the road ahead is riddled with challenges.

For blockchain to become a comprehensive solution against counterfeiting in the textile and fashion industry, it requires wider industry acceptance, deeper regulatory understanding, and technological advancements that can fuse seamlessly with existing systems. The ability to standardize blockchain integration across supply chains will also play a definitive role in its ultimate success.

The magnitude of this challenge is stark. Yet, if industry players can come together, embrace change and invest in the integration of these emerging technologies, a future-defined by premium authentic craftsmanship, nurtured by technology and devoid of the counterfeit menace could be within our grasp.

Chapter 7. Blockchain and Intellectual Property: Protecting Designs in the Digital Age

In the current global landscape, intellectual property (IP) has grown to be one of the most valuable assets for any business - and the textile and design industry is no exception. Evidently, the protection of designs, new technologies and unique techniques stands as a prerequisite to maintaining a competitive edge. Now, imagine a technology that can eradicate ambiguity, increase incontestability and warrant the rightful recognition for a design. Cue Blockchain.

Blockchain, in its most fundamental premise, is an open, transparent, and secure online ledger far removed from central governance. Being simultaneously distributable yet immutable, it creates an entirely novel paradigm for tracking, recording, and verifying transactions. But how, you might ask, is this technology relevant in the context of intellectual property protection in the increasingly digital realm of textile design?

7.1. Blockchain Unravelled: Delving Into the Basics

To understand Blockchain's applicability to IP rights, let's first break down the technology's primary components. Blockchain is essentially a growing list of records or 'blocks', linked and secured using cryptography. Each block contains a cryptographic hash of the previous block, transaction data, and a timestamp.

When a transaction occurs, it forms part of a new block. This block is linked to the preceding blocks, forming a chain. Because of the cryptographic links and the decentralized validation process, altering any information within the existed blocks becomes practically impossible. Hence, the assurance of authenticity and incorruptibility.

7.2. Applying Blockchain to Intellectual Property

The immediate vitality of Blockchain in the context of intellectual property lies in its ability to establish provenance or chronology of creations. A designer can register his design or technique on the Blockchain, thus ensuring time-stamped proof of original creation. This fundamentally solves the age-old issue plaguing creators worldwide - proving they were 'first'.

Moreover, the transparency of the technology provides an infallible testament to the IP rights, reducing disputes and enhancing the enforcement of these rights. This could mean significant cost and time savings for IP owners, improving the ease and effectiveness of protection.

7.3. A Game-Changer for Copyright

As of today, proving the ownership of a design is notoriously challenging. But, what if the designer could have irrefutable evidence of his creation when he needs it? Blockchain's potential in combatting copyright issues lies not only in evidencing the creation and ownership, but also in preventing unauthorized duplication and usage.

Each 'block' could store specifics of the creation - the design file, details of the creator, time and location of creation, etc. Once this is added to the Blockchain, the design then has a unique, unalterable digital identity, preventing misappropriation and recognizing the rightful owner.

7.4. A New Reality for Trademark

Blockchain has the potential to be a disruptive force in the field of trademarking. Trademarks serve to protect brand identity, and Blockchain's transparent and immutable nature could make the verification and protection of brand identity more easily achievable.

Furthermore, Blockchain can ensure global uniqueness of a trademark. Contrary to existing structures that require extensive research and due diligence in multiple jurisdictions, Blockchain can perhaps enable an all-encompassing, global registry of trademarks.

7.5. Patents and Beyond

Similarly, patents can be registered and maintained on a Blockchain ledger, providing an accessible and permanent record of invention. This will not only facilitate identification of patent owners and infringement cases but also streamline the patent application process itself.

Moreover, inventors can consider 'smart contracts' on the Blockchain to protect their inventions. Supposing an inventor leases the patented technique to a manufacturer, a smart contract can ensure compliance with the agreement by monitoring use against conditions and triggering penalties or cessations if violated.

7.6. Navigating the Roadblocks

Despite the vast potential, implementing Blockchain for IP protection in textiles and designs presents challenges. There loom questions around harmonizing standards, governments' acceptance, and infrastructure compatibility among such. However, weighted against the potential solutions it offers, these roadblocks reinforce rather than negate the need for Blockchain development.

Blockchain stands poised to not only simplify the mechanisms of registering and enforcing IP rights but also to enhance their clarity, integrity, and accessibility. This potentiality is all the more critical given the surge of digital design innovation in the textile industry.

As designers initiate a digital revolution in textiles, Blockchain may be the categorical instrument offering unprecedented ways to protect their ingenuity. The promise is enormous; the stage is set. It's time we weave this transformative technology into the fabric of our IP systems.

Chapter 8. Textile Traceability: Ensuring Quality from Weave to Wardrobe

The rapid progression and infiltration of technology into various sectors has brought forth unforeseen transformations and possibilities. One such exemplar is the use of Blockchain technology to ensure quality and traceability in the textile sector, extending all the way from the weave to the wardrobe.

In essence, Blockchain is a continually growing ledger system that records transactions across a network of computers in a transparent, permanent, and verifiable manner. By providing an irrefutable bedrock of data, it endows textiles with an uncanny ability to trace origins, ensure quality control, and foster a greater sense of responsibility and accountability within the supply chain.

8.1. The Essence of Textile Traceability

Textile traceability refers to the ability to track and verify a textile product's lifecycle - from raw material sourcing, production, distribution, to its retail sale or eventual disposal. This process ensures transparency and accountability in terms of environmental and social impacts. It also fosters better information exchange, leading directly to quality assurance and improved customer trust.

Traditional traceability methods required extensive human resources and depended heavily on physical documentation. This rendered them prone to errors, fraudulent alterations, and inefficiencies. However, Blockchain revolutionizes this process, providing an unalterable digital ledger, enabling easy tracking, verification and recording of a textile's journey from its place of origin to the consumer's hand.

8.2. Blockchain Unspun: How It Works

To understand the use of Blockchain in securing the quality of textiles, one must first grasp the echelons of this technology. At its core, a Blockchain is composed of a sequence of blocks, which are essentially digital information stored in a public database. Each block consists of transaction data, a timestamp, and a cryptographic hash or unique identification code.

Upon the completion of a transaction - textile production stages, for instance - it is translated into a block. The block is then broadcasted to all nodes on the Blockchain network where it is verified and added to the chain in a linear, chronological order. This method ensures that information once entered into the Blockchain cannot be tampered with, thereby ensuring the integrity of data.

8.3. Implementing Blockchain: Potential Challenges

Despite its considerable potential, implementing Blockchain technology in textiles is not without challenges. Chief among these are the lack of standardized tagging method for physical goods in the digital realm, integration with existing legacy systems, getting all stakeholders to adopt this technology uniformly, privacy concerns, and regulatory issues.

However, these issues are not insurmountable. The integration of Blockchain technology with IoT devices, such as RFIDs and smart tags, could aid in seamless translation of physical goods into digital assets. Likewise, peer-to-peer network encouragement and governmental support could foster wider adoption.

8.4. Environment and Ethics: A Symbiotic Bond

One of the most significant reasons for implementing Blockchain in textiles is the compelling case of environment and ethics. By enabling transparent traceability of materials, Blockchain allows the verification of eco-friendly farming practices, ethically sourced production, and adherence to safety norms. This supports manufacturers in asserting their green credentials and customers in making informed and conscious buying decisions.

8.5. The Role of Smart Contracts

Smart Contracts are self-executing contracts with the terms of the agreement between buyer and seller being directly written into lines of code. When applied to the textile industry, they can help automate numerous transactional processes, improving efficiency and reducing dependencies on intermediaries.

For instance, a Smart Contract can trigger automatic payment upon the fulfillment of conditions like successful delivery of raw materials or final products, ensuring timeliness and improving overall supply chain fluidity.

8.6. The Power of Provenance

Provenance is the quality of being trusted and believed in. In the context of the textile industry, Blockchain-powered provenance involves tracking and authenticating the origins and life cycle of a product. The integrity of data provided by Blockchain allows customers to trace the entire journey of a product, from the source to sale, ensuring its genuineness and sustainability credentials.

8.7. Summing Up: The Positive Impact of Blockchain

In summary, utilising Blockchain for ensuring quality from weave to wardrobe has manifold positive implications. It validates claims of sustainability, guarantees transparency, enhances traceability, enables genuine provenance, automates processes via Smart Contracts and essentially fosters a more ethical and environmentally conscious textile industry.

This technology holds great promise in regenerating trust in the textile industry's operations and ethos, leading to better consumer confidence and a more sustainable and just industrial future. Embracing Blockchain is no longer a choice; it is a move towards ensuring quality, sustainability, and positive change in the textile industry. As we continue exploring this pioneering junction where style meets substance, and authenticity meets technology, Blockchain will inevitably play a central role in fashioning our future.

Chapter 9. Fashioning Consumer Trust: Enhanced Responsibility through Blockchain

Blockchain technology was devised as a public transactional ledger for the now apparently epoch making cryptocurrency Bitcoin. Yet, it holds the potential to be far more than the backbone of a digital equivalent of the financial sector. One such industry where Blockchain can wield transformative power is the textile and fashion sector, particularly in the realm of consumer trust.

The customer's journey in the fashion industry is not one that is typically associated with transparency, traceability, and accountability. It's more often a tactfully drafted narrative designed to trigger the emotional triggers - an amalgamation of lifestyle images, crafted brand values and perceived quality. But, in our digitally evolved world, this one-way narrative is undergoing a radical shift.

9.1. Trust: The New Brand Currency

The 21st-century consumer, bolstered by an increasing digital literacy and the rising concern for issues such as sustainability and corporate ethics, craves transparency. They want to understand the lifecycle journey of their garments, from raw material sourcing to manufacturing and sale. Trust is now a valuable currency for these conscious consumers. It is cemented by transparency, responsibility, and ethical practices, not mere emotional narratives.

The objective is not simply to communicate where a garment was made and by whom, but to validate these statements. The trust deficit between consumer and producer makes Blockchain technology a potentially important tool — through its ledger system, every stage of a product's lifecycle could be documented and verified.

9.2. Blockchain: A Transparency Tool

Blockchain, at its heart, offers a transparent, immutable, and democratic platform containing a chain of transactional data. Each transaction or 'block' is documented in a public ledger, following a stringent verification process. Blockchain's decentralized nature allows multiple participants to validate transactions without the need for intermediaries, making it virtually impossible to manipulate data. This integrity and transparency hold the potential to infiltrate the opacity of the fashion supply chain, aligning with the principles of trust, security, and transparency.

9.3. A Transparent Supply Chain

Understanding blockchain's role in enhancing responsibility begins with examining the textile supply chain. This complex network, replete with manufacturers, suppliers, and retailers, harbors shady practices and ambiguous sources. Blockchain technology can simplify, illuminate and streamline this chain.

Each step in the production process, from cotton picking to garment manufacturing can be recorded as a unique 'block' in a blockchain. This digital ledger offers consumers an indisputable verification source to trace the product's origin, it establishes a clear sequence of custody and elucidates the ethics of manufacturers.

9.4. The Ethical Side of Fashion

A blockchain's ability to foster transparency and improve traceability maps directly onto ethical fashion. Consumers can now verify whether a brand that advertises itself as 'sustainable' truly complies with these principles. Right from ensuring the use of organic cotton to the adherence to fair pay and working conditions, blockchain acts as an open book recounting authentic tales.

This enhanced responsibility impacts not only the end-consumer but also encourages brands to hold their supply chain accountable. Reckless practices such as unlawful labor or environmentally harmful processes can no longer be shrouded in the enigmatic air of terms and conditions. Blockchain thrusts these practices into the spotlight, necessitating brands to take accountability for their entire production line.

9.5. Future Implications and Challenges

While the advantages of blockchain in establishing an ethically reliable fashion industry are substantial, its penetration has been minimal so far, primarily due to the complexities and costs involved. However, it's evident that as technology evolves, blockchain applications within the industry will become not just feasible but necessary.

Full adoption of blockchain will necessitate a radical reconfiguration of the fashion industry — from tracking individual raw material threads to the final product sale. Standardizing data across various entities in the supply chain poses a gargantuan challenge. Yet, if achieved, it could lead to a democratically transparent platform empowering consumers to make informed decisions, increasing brand responsibility, and potentially reshaping the textile and fashion industry for the future.

On balance, blockchain technology, with its promise of transparency, traceability, and democratic accountability, may well unlock a path towards a more ethical and reliable fashion industry; one where the solidity of trust triumphs over the whims of transient trends.

Chapter 10. The Designer's Tool: Blockchain's Influence on Creativity and Collaboration

In the age of digitalization, craftsmanship has seamlessly merged with technology, inspiring innovation at every turn. The impact of this symbiosis is palpely evident in the sphere of design and fashion, an undeniable testament to the expansive potential of technology, most notably Blockchain.

10.1. The Digital Craftsmen's Workbench: Blockchain

Blockchain's fundamental premise is driven by transparency, immutability, and decentralization. These characteristics are setting the stage for a new dimension in creativity and collaboration within the design and fashion industry. Blockchain is akin to a digital ledger, a virtual craftsmen's workbench, if you will, where each transaction or 'block' is linked in a chain that is chronologically irreversible.

The implications of such transparent technology stretch far and wide. For creative minds within the design industry, used to facing challenges around intellectual property, plagiarism, and duplication, it offers an unforeseen sense of security and identification. By recording each design in the Blockchain, it associates the design with the creator irrefutably, legitimizing their artwork while discouraging duplicity that is rampant within the industry.

10.2. From Ideas to Fashion Runways: Blockchain as a Collaborative Medium

Moreover, Blockchain also facilitates mighty collaboration opportunities. The secure and organized nature of this technology allows creators across geographic boundaries to unite. By recording individual contributions within the Blockchain, it serves as an effective medium for global collaboration, fostering an environment where ideas shared, brainstormed, developed, and finally brought to fruition in a transparent, systematic way without a fear of being overlooked.

When it comes to the fashion industry, the global supply chain has been a recurrent issue. Blockchain can effectively streamline the process by tracking not just transactions but processes and contributions. From the cotton farmer to the runway designer, each person can be acknowledged for their role, compensating them adequately, and, perhaps more importantly, fairly, giving a concrete sense of meaning to ethical fashion.

10.3. The Trust Factor: Authenticating Origin and Quality

In an era of fast fashion and knock-off designs, customers yearn not just for unique designs, but also Origin and quality assurance. Blockchain's transparent nature aids in certifying a product's authenticity and origin by following the product through its lifecycle, from its inception idea and materials used, up to its delivery to the customer. Therefore, it instills a sense of trust in customers, providing them with a means to verify the genuineness of the product.

Blockchain-supported platforms like Provenance, for instance, enable businesses to build trust with their consumers by giving them transparent access to a product's journey and history. Designers and fashion houses can also benefit from such platforms, assuring customers of their commitment to quality and ethics, and gaining their trust in return.

10.4. Smart Contracts: The Future of Licensing and Royalties

Smart contracts are another innovative application of Blockchain technology, bringing a huge shift to licensing processes within creative industries. Originating as computer codes running on top of blockchain, they are digital contracts that automatically execute and enforce the terms agreed upon by the parties involved. This eliminates the need for a middleman or an enforcing authority.

For designers, this means a more secure, efficient, and transparent way of negotiating terms and conditions for design licensing and royalty agreements. With everything recorded on the Blockchain, both parties have a clear understanding of their responsibilities, and any infringements can easily be tracked and addressed.

The global reach of Blockchain also opens the door for international licensing, a concept relatively more challenging in the traditional system. Suppose a designer in London wants to license their designs to a fashion house in Japan. In such scenarios, smart contracts can easily facilitate cross-border agreements, making the process swift and seamless.

10.5. Evolving Consumerism: Blockchain and Customization

On a final note, Blockchain's transparent nature is empowering consumers like never before. The 'demand and supply' dynamic is witnessing a trend shift, and consumers have started becoming an active part of the production chain.

Blockchain's capacity to record individual preferences and creations could give rise to a new era of personalization and customization, tailoring products to individual tastes and styles. This could spearhead a revolution, pushing designers to think from a more customer-centric perspective, thereby fuelling innovation and creativity.

The series of innovative applications that Blockchain brings to the table is exhaustive and transformative. With this technology at their disposal, designers now have a dynamic tool that fosters creativity, facilitates collaboration, and reshapes customer-oriented strategies. As the fashion and design industry take significant strides towards embracing Blockchain, the only thing certain is that this disruptive technology is stitching together a brighter and more promising future for the world of fashion and design.

The chapters that follow will delve deeper into these transformations. From the revolutionized supply chains and ethical fashion to empowered consumers and futuristic licensing processes, we'll examine the manifold implications of Blockchain in the world of design and textiles, unwinding the vibrant tapestry of innovation that it has to offer.

Chapter 11. The Future of Fashion: Forecasting Blockchain's Long-term Impact

A dawn of a new era is whispering its arrival, where the forms and functionalities of fashion could see profound transformations. The catalyst? A technology known as blockchain.

11.1. Unraveling the Power of Blockchain

Blockchain, a term tossed around often in tech corridors, finds its roots in the digital currency, bitcoin. Contrary to common misconceptions, blockchain isn't just about cryptocurrency; its potential is far more vast and significant. Simply put, a blockchain is a type of database that stores information digitally in 'blocks' which are chained together chronologically. Once a block is added to the chain, it becomes remarkably difficult to alter. This feature breeds transparency and trust through easy traceability - attributes that are of immense value to numerous industries, including fashion.

Imagine purchasing a silk blouse. With blockchain, you could potentially track every step of its journey - from silkworm to the storefront. This kind of granular data contributes to a transparent, verifiable supply chain, fostering greater trust and confidence among consumers. Moreover, it provides brands a strategic lens through which they could monitor and tweak their operations meticulously.

11.2. Blockchain's Current Infiltration in Fashion

Even in its nascence, blockchain is demonstrating its transformative potential in reshaping the fashion industry. Consumers are increasingly calling for ethical practices, and the fashion industry must deliver on this to maintain customer loyalty. For instance, Provenance - a blockchain-based platform - has piloted a project using blockchain to track the trade of raw materials in the fashion industry. It offers transparency from the source to node of every fabric woven into a garment, infusing the much-needed visibility in the journey clothes undertake.

Another example is the utilization of blockchain technology in combating counterfeit luxury items, a perennial problem in the fashion industry. Companies like Vechain and Arianee are using blockchain to ensure authenticity and ownership, offering consumers confidence that their products are genuine.

11.3. Blockchain's Foreseen Impacts and Trends

Blockchain's promise in the fashion domain is not confined to the present but extends to the future, offering revolutionary possibilities. Here are some of the long-term impacts that could result from the interweaving of blockchain with the fashion industry:

1. **Enhanced transparency:** The relevance of transparency will only escalate with time, further urging industries to adopt blockchain. Harnessing the capabilities of blockchain, fashion enterprises can track and authenticate their processes, materials, and labor involved, thus showing commitment to responsible practices.

2. **Personal ownership records:** By catering to the increasing demand for individualism and uniqueness, owners of rare fashion creations can validate their ownership using blockchain. This could pave the way for a new norm of possession records for differentiated fashion accessories and attire.

3. **Retail resurgence:** Instead of eroding physical retail, blockchain could revitalize the shopping experience by implementing smart contracts and automatic transactions, reducing human error and improving operational efficiency.

4. **Sustainable production modes:** With more precise information available, companies can make informed decisions about resource allocation, potentially reducing waste and driving sustainability in fashion production.

11.4. Overcoming the Challenges

As with any new technology, blockchain implementation in fashion also comes with its set of challenges such as the complexity of technology, need for industry-wide collaboration, and increased upfront costs. It is vital, therefore, for both fashion enterprises and technology providers to tackle these obstacles head-on and foster an understanding of the long-term gains.

11.5. Conclusion

The impending marriage of blockchain and fashion signals a meticulously woven tapestry of innovation, authenticity, and future potential. Although this union might be in its early stages, the anticipated permutations of this confluence offer a tantalizing glimpse into the future of fashion. Blockchain is the quiet current of change, and as it interlaces with the threads of the fashion industry, it promises to knit a fabric of revolution woven with sustainability, transparency, and vibrantly radical redesigns. This brave new world of fashion technology awaits with open arms, and only time will reveal the mesmerizing patterns it will unfurl.